600+ Chat GPT Prompts
for Social Media Marketing Success

600+ Chat GPT Prompts for Social Media Marketing Success is an essential guidebook designed to revolutionize your social media marketing strategies. Packed with a comprehensive collection of thought-provoking prompts, this book empowers marketers, entrepreneurs, and social media enthusiasts to create engaging and effective content that drives results.

In today's digital age, social media platforms have become indispensable tools for businesses to connect with their target audience. However, crafting compelling content that captures attention, sparks conversations, and converts followers into customers can be a challenging task. This is where "600+ Chat GPT Prompts for Social Media Marketing Success" comes to your rescue.

This book presents a wide array of meticulously crafted prompts that have been intelligently curated to cover various aspects of social media marketing. Each prompt is carefully constructed to stimulate creativity and encourage dynamic interactions with your audience across popular platforms such as Facebook, Twitter, Instagram, LinkedIn, and more.

Whether you're a seasoned social media marketer or just starting your journey, "600+ Chat GPT Prompts for Social Media Marketing Success" offers something for everyone. The prompts are conveniently organized into different categories, including:

Content Creation: Generate compelling ideas for blog posts, videos, infographics, and interactive content that captivate your audience and drive engagement.

Branding and Storytelling: Craft a strong brand identity by developing narratives, sharing customer success stories, and creating memorable experiences.

Audience Engagement: Initiate meaningful conversations, conduct surveys, and encourage user-generated content to foster a loyal and interactive community.

nfluencer Collaboration: Discover effective strategies to collaborate with influencers, create partnerships, and harness their influence to amplify your brand's reach.

Sales and Conversions: Utilize persuasive prompts to drive sales, encourage click-throughs, and boost conversion rates on your social media channels.

Analytics and Optimization: Leverage data-driven prompts to monitor your social media performance, analyze trends, and optimize your campaigns for maximum impact.

With "600+ Chat GPT Prompts for Social Media Marketing Success" in your arsenal, you'll never run out of ideas or inspiration to create compelling social media content that resonates with your audience. Gain a competitive edge, enhance your brand's visibility, and elevate your social media marketing game to new heights.

Unlock the true potential of social media marketing with this indispensable resource and embark on a journey towards social media success!

SOCIAL MEDIA STRATEGY DEVELOPMENT

SOCIAL MEDIA CONTENT CREATION

SOCIAL MEDIA ADVERTISING

SOCIAL MEDIA ANALYTICS AND METRICS

SOCIAL MEDIA LISTENING & MONITORING

SOCIAL MEDIA MANAGEMENT AND SCHEDULING TOOLS

INFLUENCER MARKETING ON SOCIAL MEDIA

VIDEO MARKETING ON SOCIAL MEDIA

FACEBOOK MARKETING

INSTAGRAM MARKETING

TWITTER MARKETING

LINKEDIN MARKETING

PINTEREST MARKETING

TIKTOK MARKETING

SNAPCHAT MARKETING

HASHTAG CAMPAIGNS ON SOCIAL MEDIA

SOCIAL MEDIA CONTESTS AND GIVEAWAYS

USER-GENERATED CONTENT (UGC) CAMPAIGNS

SOCIAL MEDIA CUSTOMER SERVICE

CRISIS MANAGEMENT AND SOCIAL MEDIA

Social Media Strategy Development

Social media strategy development is the process of creating a plan to use social media platforms, such as Facebook, Instagram, and Twitter, to achieve specific goals.

This plan includes things like determining which platforms to use, identifying the target audience, deciding what type of content to post, and establishing how often to post.

The strategy is designed to help businesses or individuals effectively engage with their audience, build brand awareness, and achieve their desired outcomes.

Prompts

- What are the key elements of a successful social media strategy?
- How do you identify and define your target audience for social media marketing?
- What role should competitive analysis play in developing a social media strategy?
- How do you choose the right social media platforms to focus on for your business?
- What types of content should you be creating for social media, and how do you ensure it's engaging?

- How can you ensure that your social media strategy aligns with your overall marketing goals?
- What is the best way to measure the effectiveness of your social media strategy?
- How do you adapt your social media strategy to changes in the industry or marketplace?
- What is the importance of setting clear objectives and goals for your social media strategy?
- What steps should you take to ensure your social media strategy is sustainable and can be maintained over time?
- How can you ensure that your social media strategy reflects your brand's values and personality?
- What are the key factors to consider when developing a social media content
- calendar?
- How do you create a social media posting schedule that maximizes engagement and reach?
- What are some effective tactics for increasing follower engagement on social media?
- How can you leverage user-generated content (UGC) in your social media strategy?
- How can you use influencer marketing to support your social media strategy?

- How do you identify the right influencers to work with for your brand?
- What is the importance of listening and responding to your audience on social media?
- How can you use social media analytics to inform and improve your social media strategy?
- What is the role of A/B testing in optimizing your social media strategy?
- How can you use social media to build brand awareness and increase visibility?
- What role should customer feedback and insights play in developing your social media strategy?
- How can you use social media to drive traffic to your website or online store?
- What are some effective tactics for lead generation on social media?
- How can you use social media to build relationships with your audience and foster customer loyalty?
- How can you create a consistent brand voice across all your social media platforms?
- How do you stay up to date with social media trends and changes?
- How can you incorporate visual content into your social media strategy for maximum impact?
- What is the importance of having a crisis management plan in place for your social media strategy?

- How can you ensure that your social media strategy is accessible and inclusive for all members of your audience?

Social Media Content Creation

Social media content creation is the process of producing and publishing material, such as text, images, or videos, specifically designed for social media platforms, to engage with the audience, increase brand awareness, and achieve marketing goals.

Prompts

- How can you ensure that your social media content is aligned with your overall marketing strategy?
- What are the different types of social media content, and when should you use each type?
- How can you create content that resonates with your target audience and encourages engagement?
- What are some best practices for creating visually appealing social media content?
- How do you determine the appropriate tone and voice for your social media content?
- What is the importance of creating a content calendar for social media, and how do you do it effectively?

- What are some creative ways to repurpose existing content for social media?
- How can you use user-generated content (UGC) to enhance your social media content?
- What role should storytelling play in your social media content strategy?
- How can you use humor effectively in your social media content?
- How do you create social media content that is inclusive and accessible to all members of your audience?
- How can you leverage social media trends and current events in your content creation?
- How do you optimize your social media content for different platforms and devices?
- What is the role of visual content in and how can you use it to tell a story or convey a message?
- What are some tips for creating compelling video content for social media?
- How can you use user personas to guide your social media content creation?
- What are some ways to make your social media content stand out in a crowded marketplace?
- What is the importance of authenticity in and how can you maintain it?
- How do you use data and analytics to inform your social media content creation strategy?

- How can you create social media content that is optimized for search engines (SEO)?
- What are some tips for creating effective social media graphics and images?
- How can you use social media to showcase your products or services?
- How can you create social media content that tells a story and evokes emotion?
- How do you write compelling social media captions that encourage engagement?
- What are some tips for creating social media content that educates and informs your audience?
- How can you use humor or storytelling to humanize your brand through social media content?
- How can you create social media content that is shareable and encourages virality?
- What are some effective ways to create social media content that is authentic and relatable to your audience?
- How can you use social media to demonstrate your company's values and social responsibility?
- What is the importance of tracking and analyzing social media metrics to evaluate the effectiveness of your content?

Social Media Advertising

Social media advertising is the act of creating and placing ads on social media platforms to reach a specific target audience with the goal of promoting a product or service, driving traffic to a website, or increasing brand awareness.

Prompts

- How can you choose the right social media platforms to advertise on based on your target audience and marketing goals?
- What are the different types of social media ads available, and when should you use each type?
- How do you set an advertising budget for your social media campaigns, and what factors should you consider?
- How can you ensure that your social media ads are visually appealing and attention-grabbing?
- What is the importance of targeting in social media advertising, and how can you do it effectively?
- What are some best practices for creating ad copy that converts on social media?
- How can you use retargeting and remarketing to increase conversions through social media advertising?

- What are some creative ways to use social media influencers in your advertising campaigns?
- How can you use A/B testing to optimize your social media ad campaigns?
- How can you measure the success of your social media advertising campaigns using analytics and metrics?
- What is the role of video in social media advertising, and how can you create effective video ads?
- How can you use social proof and customer reviews in your social media advertising campaigns?
- What are some tips for creating mobile-friendly social media ads?
- How can you use social media advertising to increase brand awareness and reach a larger audience?
- What are some effective ways to use targeting options such as location, interests, and behaviors in your social media ads?
- How can you use Facebook Ads Manager to manage and optimize your social media advertising campaigns?
- What are some ways to create ads that are personalized to individual users on social media?
- How can you use social media advertising to drive traffic to your website or landing page?

- How can you use social media advertising to promote sales, discounts, and special offers?
- What are some common mistakes to avoid when creating social media ads?
- How can you create social media ads that are consistent with your brand image and messaging?
- What is the importance of ad relevance and quality score in social media advertising?
- How can you use Instagram Stories ads to promote your brand or products?
- How can you create effective call-to-action (CTA) buttons in your social media ads?
- What are some ways to create urgency in your social media advertising campaigns?
- How can you use Twitter Ads to reach a larger audience and increase engagement?
- What are some tips for creating engaging and interactive social media ads?
- How can you use LinkedIn Ads to target a professional audience and increase brand awareness?
- How can you use Pinterest Ads to promote your products or services and drive traffic to your website?
- What are some best practices for creating successful social media advertising campaigns across multiple platforms?

Social Media Analytics and Metrics

Social media analytics and metrics refer to the collection and analysis of data from social media platforms, such as likes, comments, shares, followers, and engagement rates. These insights help measure the effectiveness of social media strategies and campaigns, track audience behaviour, and identify areas for improvement.

Prompts

- What are the most important social media metrics to track, and why?
- How can you use social media analytics to better understand your target audience and their behaviours?
- What are some common social media analytics tools, and how do they differ?
- How can you measure the effectiveness of your social media marketing campaigns using metrics such as reach, engagement, and conversions?
- What are some best practices for tracking and analysing social media metrics in real-time?
- How can you use social media analytics to identify trends and changes in your industry?
- How can you use social media metrics to monitor your brand's reputation and sentiment?

- What are some tips for setting measurable social media goals and objectives?
- How can you use social media analytics to optimize your content strategy and increase engagement?
- What are some ways to use social media analytics to identify your top-performing content and replicate its success?
- How can you use social media metrics to measure the ROI of your social media marketing efforts?
- What are some best practices for creating social media reports that effectively
- communicate your results and insights?
- How can you use social media analytics to monitor your competitors' activities and strategies?
- What are some ways to measure the impact of your social media advertising campaigns using analytics?
- How can you use social media analytics to identify and target your most valuable customer segments?
- How can you use social media metrics to track the effectiveness of your customer service efforts?
- What are some tips for analysing social media metrics to uncover actionable insights?
- How can you use social media analytics to identify and address customer complaints or issues?

- What are some ways to use social media metrics to optimize your paid social media campaigns?
- How can you use social media analytics to identify and engage with influencers in your industry?
- What are some best practices for measuring the effectiveness of your social media customer acquisition efforts?
- How can you use social media analytics to identify and address customer churn?
- What are some ways to use social media metrics to optimize your social media content calendar?
- How can you use social media analytics to identify and capitalize on emerging trends and topics?
- What are some tips for using social media analytics to measure the impact of your social media customer loyalty efforts?
- How can you use social media metrics to measure the effectiveness of your social media customer support efforts?
- What are some best practices for tracking social media metrics across multiple platforms?
- How can you use social media analytics to identify the most effective social media channels for your business?
- What are some ways to use social media metrics to improve your overall customer experience?

Social Media Listening & Monitoring

Social media listening and monitoring is the practice of tracking and analysing conversations and mentions about a brand, product, or topic on social media platforms. This helps businesses or individuals understand what their audience is saying about them, identify potential issues or opportunities, and adjust their social media strategies accordingly.

Prompts

- What is social media listening, and why is it important for businesses?
- How can social media listening help you understand your customers' needs and preferences?
- What are some common social media monitoring tools, and how do they differ?
- How can you use social media listening to monitor your brand's reputation and respond to customer feedback?
- What are some best practices for setting up social media monitoring for your business?
- How can you use social media listening to identify and address customer complaints or issues?
- What are some ways to use social media monitoring to keep track of your competitors' activities and strategies?

- How can you use social media listening to identify and engage with influencers in your industry?
- What are some tips for analyzing social media conversations to uncover actionable insights?
- How can you use social media monitoring to stay up-to-date on industry trends and topics?
- What are some ways to use social media listening to identify and capitalize on emerging trends and topics?
- How can you use social media monitoring to identify potential sales leads and opportunities?
- What are some best practices for responding to customer feedback and complaints on social media?
- How can you use social media listening to improve your overall customer experience?
- What are some ways to use social media monitoring to improve your customer service efforts?
- How can you use social media listening to identify and address potential crisis situations?
- What are some tips for using social media monitoring to stay on top of brand mentions and conversations?
- How can you use social media listening to identify and address potential legal or regulatory issues?

- What are some ways to use social media monitoring to identify and address fake or misleading information about your brand?
- How can you use social media listening to identify and address potential security or privacy issues?
- What are some best practices for using social media listening to gather customer feedback and insights?
- How can you use social media monitoring to identify and address potential social media policy violations?
- What are some ways to use social media listening to gather competitive intelligence?
- How can you use social media monitoring to measure the effectiveness of your social media marketing campaigns?
- What are some tips for using social media listening to identify and address potential employee issues?
- How can you use social media monitoring to identify and address potential online harassment or bullying?
- What are some ways to use social media listening to stay up-to-date on industry news and developments?
- How can you use social media monitoring to identify and address potential customer privacy concerns?
- What are some best practices for setting up alerts and notifications for social media monitoring?

- How can you use social media listening to continuously improve and refine your social media marketing strategy?

Social Media Management and Scheduling Tools

Social media management and scheduling tools are software programs designed to help businesses or individuals manage their social media accounts more efficiently. These tools allow users to schedule posts in advance, monitor multiple accounts in one place, and analyze engagement data. This helps save time, streamline the social media process, and improve overall social media strategy.

Prompts

- What are some of the most popular social media management tools available?
- How do social media management tools help businesses streamline their social media marketing efforts?
- What are the benefits of using social media scheduling tools?
- What features should you look for in a social media management tool?
- How do social media scheduling tools help businesses save time?
- What are some of the best social media management tools for small businesses?

- How can social media management tools help you measure your social media marketing ROI?
- What are the best social media management tools for managing multiple social media accounts?
- How do social media scheduling tools help you maintain a consistent posting schedule?
- What are the benefits of using a social media management tool with built-in analytics?
- How do social media management tools help you track your social media engagement?
- What are some of the most popular social media scheduling tools available?
- How can social media management tools help you respond to customer inquiries and comments more efficiently?
- What are some of the best social media management tools for scheduling posts across multiple platforms?
- How do social media management tools help businesses stay organized and on top of their social media marketing efforts?
- What are some of the most important factors to consider when choosing a social media management tool?
- How can social media scheduling tools help businesses ensure they post at the optimal times?

- What are the advantages of using social media management tools with team collaboration features?
- How do social media management tools help businesses stay on top of industry trends and news?
- What are some of the best social media management tools for businesses with limited resources?
- What are some of the most popular free social media management tools available?
- How do social media management tools help businesses increase their social media engagement?
- What are some of the most important features of a social media management tool for tracking brand mentions and sentiment?
- How can social media scheduling tools help businesses maintain a consistent brand voice?
- What are the advantages of using a social media management tool with automated reporting features?
- How do social media management tools help businesses manage their social media reputation?
- What are the best social media management tools for businesses with a global presence?
- How can social media scheduling tools help businesses stay on top of seasonal promotions and events?

- What are some of the best social media management tools for businesses in highly regulated industries?
- How do social media management tools help businesses stay on top of their social media advertising efforts?

Influencer Marketing on Social Media

Influencer marketing on social media is a type of advertising where a brand partners with an individual who has a large following on social media platforms such as Instagram, YouTube, or TikTok. The influencer creates content featuring the brand or product and shares it with their audience, typically receiving compensation for the collaboration. The goal is to increase brand awareness, reach a new audience, and drive sales through the influencer's followers.

Prompts

- What is influencer marketing and how does it work on social media platforms?
- How to identify the right influencer for your brand on social media?
- What are the benefits of using influencer marketing on social media for your business?

- How to negotiate with an influencer for collaboration on social media?
- How to measure the success of your influencer marketing campaigns on social media?
- How to create an effective influencer marketing strategy for social media?
- What types of content work best for influencer marketing on social media?
- How to leverage influencer-generated content on social media for your brand?
- What are the common mistakes to avoid in influencer marketing on social media?
- How to comply with FTC guidelines for influencer marketing on social media?
- How to set a budget for your influencer marketing campaigns on social media?
- How to track ROI and conversions from your influencer marketing campaigns on social media?
- How to build long-term relationships with influencers on social media for your brand?
- What are the best practices for reaching out to influencers on social media?
- How to integrate influencer marketing with your overall social media strategy?
- What are the legal considerations for influencer marketing on social media?
- How to use micro-influencers to reach a niche audience on social media?
- How to measure the engagement rate of influencers on social media?

- How to create a successful affiliate marketing program with influencers on social media?
- How to collaborate with influencers for cross-promotion on social media?
- What are the different types of influencers on social media and how to work with each one?
- How to manage your relationships with multiple influencers on social media?
- How to leverage user-generated content with influencer marketing on social media?
- How to use influencer marketing on social media to increase brand awareness?
- What are the ethical considerations in influencer marketing on social media?
- How to create a contract for influencer marketing collaborations on social media?
- How to leverage the power of influencers to drive sales on social media?
- What are the best tools to use for influencer research and outreach on social media?
- How to use data analytics to optimize your influencer marketing campaigns on social media?
- How to develop a long-term influencer marketing strategy on social media?

Video Marketing on Social Media

Video marketing on social media involves creating and sharing videos on social media platforms, such as Facebook, Instagram, or YouTube, to promote a brand, product, or service. These videos can take various forms, such as ads, tutorials, how-to videos, or behind-the-scenes footage. The goal is to engage with the audience, increase brand awareness, and drive traffic to a website or landing page.

Prompts

- What are the benefits of using video marketing on social media?
- How do you choose the right social media platform for your video marketing campaign?
- What are some effective video marketing strategies for social media?
- How can you optimize your videos for social media platforms?
- What are some best practices for creating engaging video content for social media?
- What role does storytelling play in video marketing on social media?
- How can you measure the success of your video marketing campaigns on social media?

- What are some common mistakes to avoid when creating video content for social media?
- How can you leverage user-generated content in your video marketing strategy on social media?
- What are some ways to repurpose video content across different social media platforms?
- How important is it to have a strong call-to-action in your social media video marketing?
- What are some creative ideas for incorporating humor into your social media video marketing?
- How can you effectively use subtitles in your social media video marketing?
- How do you ensure that your social media video content is mobile-friendly?
- What are some tips for creating videos that will stand out on crowded social media feeds?
- How can you use video influencers to boost your social media video marketing efforts?
- What are some trends in social media video marketing that businesses should be aware of?
- How can you use live video on social media to engage with your audience?
- What are some ways to incorporate storytelling into your social media video marketing strategy?

- How can you use video to build trust and authority with your social media audience?
- What are some effective ways to distribute your social media videos to reach a wider audience?
- How can you use social media analytics to inform your video marketing strategy?
- What are some best practices for creating videos that are shareable on social media?
- How can you use video to showcase your products or services on social media?
- What are some tips for optimizing your social media video content for search engines?
- How can you use video to humanize your brand on social media?
- What are some ways to incorporate customer testimonials into your social media video marketing?
- How can you use video to showcase your company culture on social media?
- What are some best practices for creating video ads on social media?
- How can you use video to educate your social media audience about your industry or niche?

Facebook Marketing

Facebook marketing is the use of Facebook's features and tools to promote a brand, product, or service. This can include creating a Facebook page, posting content, running ads, and using analytics to track performance.

The goal is to engage with the audience, build brand awareness, and achieve marketing objectives on the Facebook platform.

Prompts

- How to set up a Facebook Business Page for your brand?
- What types of content work best for Facebook marketing?
- How to create engaging posts for your Facebook Business Page?
- How to optimize your Facebook Business Page for search engines?
- How to use Facebook Insights to track your Page's performance?
- What are the different types of Facebook Ads available?
- How to set up and run Facebook Ads for your brand?
- What targeting options are available for Facebook Ads?
- How to create compelling ad copy for Facebook Ads?

- How to design effective visuals for Facebook Ads?
- How to track and analyse the performance of your Facebook Ads?
- How to use Facebook Live to connect with your audience?
- How to create a Facebook Group for your brand?
- How to use Facebook Groups for community building and engagement?
- How to manage your Facebook Page's messaging inbox efficiently?
- How to respond to negative comments and reviews on your Facebook Page?
- How to use Facebook Events to promote your brand's activities?
- How to use Facebook Messenger for customer support and lead generation?
- How to integrate Facebook marketing with your overall digital marketing strategy?
- How to leverage user-generated content for Facebook marketing?
- How to collaborate with influencers on Facebook marketing campaigns?
- How to use Facebook's ad manager effectively?
- How to create custom audiences for your Facebook Ads?
- How to set up and track Facebook pixel for retargeting?
- How to use Facebook's Lookalike audience to expand your reach?

- How to use Facebook's lead generation ads to capture leads?
- How to measure the ROI of your Facebook marketing efforts?
- How to stay up-to-date with Facebook's changing algorithm and policies? ▪ How to run successful A/B tests for your Facebook Ads?
- How to use Facebook as a customer research tool?

Instagram Marketing

Instagram marketing is the use of Instagram's features and tools to promote a brand, product, or service.

This can include creating an Instagram profile, posting content, using hashtags, collaborating with influencers, and running ads.

The goal is to engage with the audience, increase brand awareness, and achieve marketing objectives on the Instagram platform.

Prompts

- How can you optimize your Instagram bio to attract more followers?
- What are some effective strategies for increasing engagement on Instagram posts?
- What types of Instagram content are most effective for driving sales?
- How can you leverage Instagram's Stories feature to promote your business?
- What are some best practices for using hashtags on Instagram?
- How can you use Instagram to build brand awareness?
- How can you use Instagram's Insights to track and analyze your performance on the platform?
- What are some tips for creating visually appealing Instagram content?
- How can you use Instagram to build a community around your brand?
- How can you use Instagram to promote your products or services?
- What are some ways to use Instagram influencers to grow your brand?
- How can you use Instagram's Shopping feature to sell products directly from your profile?
- What are some strategies for gaining more Instagram followers?

- What are some best practices for creating Instagram ads?
- How can you use Instagram to drive traffic to your website or blog?
- What are some ways to use Instagram to connect with your audience?
- What are some creative ways to use Instagram's video features?
- How can you measure the success of your Instagram marketing efforts?
- How can you use Instagram to promote events or launches?
- What are some tips for creating effective Instagram captions?
- What are some strategies for leveraging user-generated content on Instagram?
- How can you use Instagram to showcase your brand's personality?
- What are some best practices for running an Instagram contest or giveaway?
- How can you use Instagram to connect with other businesses or influencers in your industry?
- What are some ways to use Instagram to showcase your products or services?
- What are some strategies for creating a consistent visual aesthetic on Instagram?
- How can you use Instagram to build relationships with your followers?
- What are some tips for using Instagram's Direct Messaging feature to connect with customers?

- How can you use Instagram to build credibility and authority in your industry?
- What are some best practices for using Instagram's advertising tools to reach your target audience?

Twitter Marketing

Twitter marketing is the use of Twitter's features and tools to promote a brand, product, or service.

This can include creating a Twitter profile, tweeting content, using hashtags, participating in Twitter chats, and running ads.
The goal is to engage with the audience, increase brand awareness, and achieve marketing objectives on the Twitter platform.

Prompts

- What are some of the key features of a successful Twitter marketing campaign?
- How can you use Twitter to build brand awareness and generate leads?
- What are some of the most effective Twitter advertising formats?
- How can you use Twitter to drive traffic to your website?

- What are the best practices for optimizing your Twitter profile for maximum engagement?
- How can you use Twitter chats to build your brand and connect with your audience?
- What are some tips for creating engaging tweets that will resonate with your target audience?
- How can you use Twitter analytics to track the success of your marketing campaigns?
- How can you use Twitter to establish thought leadership and credibility in your industry?
- What are some common mistakes to avoid when marketing on Twitter?
- How can you use Twitter's targeting options to reach your ideal audience?
- How can you use Twitter to provide customer support and improve your customer experience?
- What are some creative ways to use Twitter to promote your products or services?
- How can you leverage Twitter influencers to increase your reach and engagement?
- How can you use Twitter to stay up-to-date on industry news and trends?
- What are some best practices for managing and growing your Twitter following?
- How can you use Twitter to promote events and engage with attendees?

- What are some effective strategies for using Twitter in B2B marketing?
- How can you use Twitter to build and maintain relationships with your customers?
- How can you use Twitter to support your overall social media marketing strategy?
- What are some ways to create a strong brand voice on Twitter?
- How can you use Twitter to conduct market research and gather customer feedback?
- What are some tips for using Twitter to engage with your audience in real-time?
- How can you use Twitter to drive sales and revenue for your business?
- What are some ways to measure the ROI of your Twitter marketing efforts?
- How can you use Twitter to build partnerships and collaborations with other businesses?
- What are some effective ways to use Twitter to recruit new talent for your company?
- How can you use Twitter to promote user-generated content and increase brand loyalty?
- What are some best practices for using Twitter to market to different age groups?
- How can you use Twitter to stay ahead of your competitors in your industry?

LinkedIn Marketing

LinkedIn marketing is the use of LinkedIn's features and tools to promote a brand, product, or service.

This can include creating a LinkedIn profile, sharing content, posting updates, running ads, and using analytics to track performance.

The goal is to engage with the audience, increase brand awareness, and achieve marketing objectives on the LinkedIn platform, which is primarily used for professional networking and career development.

Prompts

- How can you optimize your LinkedIn profile to attract more clients or customers?
- What is the ideal length for LinkedIn posts?
- How can you use LinkedIn to establish yourself as a thought leader in your industry?
- How can you use LinkedIn groups to build your network and increase engagement with your content?
- What is the best way to leverage LinkedIn's messaging feature for business development?

- How can you use LinkedIn's Sales Navigator to generate leads and prospects for your business?
- What are some best practices for creating effective LinkedIn ads?
- What are the key metrics to track when measuring the success of your LinkedIn advertising campaigns?
- How can you use LinkedIn to recruit top talent for your company?
- What are some strategies for building a strong LinkedIn company page?
- How can you use LinkedIn's publishing platform to share long-form content with your network?
- How can you use LinkedIn video to increase engagement with your content?
- What are some tips for creating eye-catching and professional-looking LinkedIn profile and cover photos?
- How can you use LinkedIn to showcase your company culture and values to potential clients or employees?
- What is the best way to approach influencer marketing on LinkedIn?
- How can you use LinkedIn to promote webinars or events related to your business?
- How can you use LinkedIn's alumni tool to find and connect with former colleagues and classmates?

- What are some effective strategies for generating more referrals on LinkedIn?
- How can you use LinkedIn to conduct market research and gather insights about your target audience?
- What are some tips for creating engaging and effective LinkedIn headlines?
- How can you use LinkedIn to expand your professional network beyond your immediate industry or field?
- What are some ways to use LinkedIn to promote your business to a global audience?
- How can you use LinkedIn to establish partnerships with other businesses or industry leaders?
- What are some ways to use LinkedIn to stay up-to-date on industry trends and news?
- How can you use LinkedIn to promote your personal brand as an entrepreneur or business leader?
- What are some best practices for engaging with your LinkedIn followers and connections?
- How can you use LinkedIn to build relationships with potential clients or customers?
- What are some common mistakes to avoid when using LinkedIn for business?

- How can you use LinkedIn to target and engage with specific segments of your target audience?
- What are some ways to measure the ROI of your LinkedIn marketing efforts?

Pinterest Marketing

Pinterest marketing is the use of Pinterest's features and tools to promote a brand, product, or service.

This can include creating a Pinterest profile, creating and sharing pins, using boards to organize content, collaborating with influencers, and running ads.

The goal is to engage with the audience, increase brand awareness, and achieve marketing objectives on the Pinterest platform, which is primarily used for visual discovery and inspiration.

Prompts

- What are the benefits of using Pinterest for your business?
- How can you create a Pinterest business account and set it up for success?
- What are the best practices for optimizing your Pinterest profile?

- What types of content perform best on Pinterest?
- How can you create eye-catching and engaging Pins?
- What are some effective strategies for increasing your Pinterest followers?
- How can you leverage Pinterest Analytics to improve your strategy?
- What are some ways to promote your Pinterest account on other social media platforms?
- How can you use Pinterest to drive traffic to your website or online store?
- What are the key elements of a successful Pinterest ad campaign?
- How can you target the right audience for your Pinterest ads?
- What types of Pinterest ads are available and which ones are right for your business?
- What are some tips for creating effective Pinterest ad creatives?
- How can you track and measure the success of your Pinterest ad campaigns?
- What are some common mistakes to avoid when advertising on Pinterest?
- How can you use Pinterest to showcase your brand's personality and voice?
- What are some effective ways to use Pinterest for customer research and feedback?
- How can you collaborate with influencers on Pinterest to reach a wider audience?

- What are some ways to build relationships with other brands on Pinterest?
- How can you use Pinterest to launch a new product or service?
- What are the best ways to optimize your Pinterest boards for search?
- How can you use Pinterest to promote seasonal or holiday campaigns?
- What are some effective ways to repurpose content on Pinterest?
- How can you use Pinterest to attract local customers?
- What are some ways to increase engagement on your Pinterest account?
- How can you use Pinterest to position your brand as an industry leader?
- What are some effective ways to use Pinterest for customer service and support?
- How can you use Pinterest to showcase user-generated content?
- What are some strategies for using Pinterest to grow your email list?
- How can you use Pinterest to stay up-to-date on industry trends and insights?

TikTok Marketing

TikTok marketing is the use of TikTok's features and tools to promote a brand, product, or service.

This can include creating a TikTok profile, creating and sharing videos, using hashtags, collaborating with influencers, and running ads. The goal is to engage with the audience, increase brand awareness, and achieve marketing objectives on the TikTok platform, which is primarily used for short-form video content.

Prompts

- PromptsWhat are the key features and benefits of TikTok for marketers?
- What types of content work well on TikTok?
- How can you identify and target your audience on TikTok?
- What are the best practices for creating engaging TikTok videos?
- How can you leverage influencer marketing on TikTok?
- How can you use hashtags effectively on TikTok?
- What are the key metrics you should track for TikTok marketing campaigns?
- How can you use TikTok ads to reach your target audience?
- What are the pros and cons of using user-generated content on TikTok?
- How can you create a TikTok marketing strategy that aligns with your brand?

- How can you collaborate with other TikTok creators for increased reach?
- What are the best practices for engaging with your audience on TikTok?
- How can you use TikTok to build brand awareness and increase brand loyalty?
- What are the dos and don'ts of TikTok marketing?
- How can you use TikTok challenges to engage your audience?
- What are the common mistakes to avoid in TikTok marketing?
- How can you measure the success of your TikTok marketing efforts?
- How can you use TikTok to drive traffic to your website or online store?
- How can you leverage TikTok's algorithm to increase reach and engagement?
- How can you create compelling captions for your TikTok videos?
- How can you use TikTok to showcase your products or services?
- What are the best practices for incorporating music into your TikTok videos?
- How can you optimize your TikTok profile for maximum visibility and engagement?
- What are the differences between organic and paid TikTok marketing strategies?
- How can you use TikTok to humanize your brand and connect with your audience?

- What are the best practices for engaging with the TikTok community?
- How can you use TikTok to stay on top of industry trends and insights?
- How can you use TikTok to support social and environmental causes?
- What are the opportunities for B2B marketing on TikTok?
- How can you use TikTok to generate leads and drive sales?

Snapchat Marketing

Snapchat marketing is the use of Snapchat's features and tools to promote a brand, product, or service.

This can include creating a Snapchat profile, creating and sharing snaps, using filters and lenses, collaborating with influencers, and running ads.

The goal is to engage with the audience, increase brand awareness, and achieve marketing objectives on the Snapchat platform, which is primarily used for sharing short-lived, ephemeral content.

Prompts

- What are the demographics of Snapchat users and how can you leverage this information to create effective marketing strategies?
- What are the different ad formats available on Snapchat and which one is most suitable for your marketing objectives?
- How can you create engaging Snapchat Stories that resonate with your target audience and drive conversions?
- What is the role of influencers in Snapchat marketing and how can you identify and collaborate with the right influencers for your brand?
- How can you use Snapchat's geofilters and lenses to increase brand awareness and engagement with your target audience?
- What are some best practices for creating effective Snapchat ads that capture the attention of users and drive action?
- How can you track and measure the effectiveness of your Snapchat marketing campaigns using analytics and insights?
- What are some creative ways to use augmented reality (AR) in your Snapchat marketing campaigns?
- How can you leverage Snapchat's Discover section to promote your brand and reach a wider audience?

- How can you create a Snapchat content strategy that aligns with your brand's values and resonates with your target audience?
- What are the best practices for creating and promoting user-generated content (UGC) on Snapchat?
- How can you use Snapchat's Snap Map feature to increase engagement with your brand and promote your products or services?
- What are some effective ways to promote your Snapchat account on other social media platforms and your website?
- How can you leverage Snapchat's Shoppable AR feature to drive sales and revenue for your brand?
- What are some common mistakes to avoid in Snapchat marketing and how can you prevent them?
- How can you create a cohesive brand identity on Snapchat that aligns with your overall marketing strategy?
- What are some effective ways to use Snapchat to promote events and engage with attendees?
- How can you use Snapchat to conduct market research and gather valuable insights about your target audience?
- What are the best practices for using Snapchat to promote new product launches and build excitement among your audience?

- How can you use Snapchat's ad targeting options to reach the right audience with your marketing messages?
- What are some creative ways to use Snapchat's Bitmoji feature in your marketing campaigns?
- How can you use Snapchat's Snap Originals to reach a wider audience and promote your brand?
- What are some effective ways to use influencer marketing on Snapchat to drive engagement and conversions?
- How can you create a Snapchat content calendar that aligns with your overall marketing goals and objectives?
- How can you use Snapchat's self-serve ad platform to create and launch effective ad campaigns on a budget?
- What are the best practices for optimizing your Snapchat ads for better performance and results?
- How can you use Snapchat to provide personalized customer service and support to your audience?
- What are some effective ways to use user-generated lenses to promote your brand on Snapchat?
- How can you use Snapchat's augmented reality (AR) technology to create interactive and engaging experiences for your audience?

- What are some effective ways to use Snapchat's ad manager to track and measure the performance of your campaigns and optimize for better results?

Hashtag Campaigns on Social Media

A hashtag campaign on social media is a marketing strategy that involves using a specific hashtag to promote a brand, product, or service.

The hashtag is used in social media posts, encouraging users to create and share their own posts using the same hashtag.

This helps to create a sense of community and promote brand awareness, as well as track user-generated content related to the campaign. The goal is to increase engagement and drive traffic to a website or landing page.

Prompts

- What is a hashtag campaign and how can it benefit your social media marketing efforts?
- How can you research and identify popular hashtags relevant to your target audience and industry?

- How can you create a unique and memorable hashtag for your campaign?
- What are the dos and don'ts of using hashtags in your social media marketing strategy?
- How can you track and measure the success of your hashtag campaign?
- What are some creative ways to incorporate hashtags into your social media posts and stories?
- How can you leverage user-generated content in your hashtag campaign to increase engagement and reach?
- How can you collaborate with influencers or other brands to amplify your hashtag campaign?
- How can you use paid social media advertising to increase the visibility of your hashtag campaign?
- How can you leverage seasonal or trending hashtags in your campaigns to increase engagement and reach?
- How can you use hashtags to promote a specific product or service in your social media marketing strategy?
- What are the best practices for using hashtags on different social media platforms, such as Twitter, Instagram, and TikTok?
- How can you localize your hashtag campaign to reach a specific audience in a particular geographic location?

- How can you encourage user participation in your hashtag campaign, such as through contests or challenges?
- How can you monitor and respond to user-generated content associated with your hashtag campaign?
- How can you use hashtags to build a community and foster brand loyalty among your social media followers?
- How can you use hashtags to promote a social cause or charitable organization?
- What are some common mistakes to avoid when running a hashtag campaign on social media?
- How can you incorporate emojis and other symbols into your hashtag campaigns to make them more visually appealing and engaging?
- How can you leverage user data and insights to refine and optimize your hashtag campaign strategy?
- How can you use hashtags to drive traffic to your website or other online platforms?
- How can you use hashtags to build your personal or brand identity and establish thought leadership in your industry?
- How can you use hashtags to attract new followers and expand your social media reach?
- How can you use hashtags to highlight and promote customer reviews and testimonials?

- How can you use hashtags to promote exclusive offers or discounts to your social media followers?
- How can you use hashtags to showcase behind-the-scenes content and give your followers a sneak peek into your brand?
- How can you use hashtags to promote industry events or trade shows that your brand is attending or sponsoring?
- How can you use hashtags to generate buzz and anticipation around a new product launch or brand announcement?
- How can you use hashtags to tell a story and create a cohesive brand narrative across your social media channels?
- How can you use hashtags to collaborate with other businesses or influencers in your industry and cross-promote each other's content?

Social Media Contests and Giveaways

Social media contests and giveaways are promotional activities that involve offering prizes or rewards to followers and users who engage with a brand's social media content.

This can include liking or sharing posts, commenting on content, or creating user-generated content using a specific hashtag.

The goal is to increase engagement, followers, and brand awareness by incentivizing users to participate in the contest or giveaway.

The winners are typically selected at random or based on a specific set of criteria, and the prizes can range from small gifts to larger rewards like cash or vacations.

Prompts

- What are some benefits of running a social media contest or giveaway for your brand?
- How can you determine the best type of contest or giveaway to run on social media for your target audience?
- What are some legal considerations you need to keep in mind when running a social media contest or giveaway?
- How can you use social media to promote your contest or giveaway effectively?
- What are some creative ideas for prizes to offer in a social media contest or giveaway?
- What are some strategies for choosing a winner for a social media contest or giveaway?
- How can you measure the success of your social media contest or giveaway?

- What are some examples of successful social media contests or giveaways, and what can you learn from them?
- How can you make your social media contest or giveaway more engaging for participants?
- What are some common mistakes to avoid when running a social media contest or giveaway?
- ▪ How can you collaborate with influencers to promote your social media contest or giveaway?
- What are some ways to keep participants engaged and interested in your social media contest or giveaway throughout its duration?
- How can you use user-generated content (UGC) in your social media contest or giveaway?
- What are some guidelines for setting rules and guidelines for a social media contest or giveaway?
- How can you use social media advertising to increase the reach and engagement of your contest or giveaway?
- How can you use email marketing to promote your social media contest or giveaway?
- How can you use hashtags to increase the visibility of your social media contest or giveaway?

- What are some ways to incorporate your brand values and messaging into your social media contest or giveaway?
- How can you make your social media contest or giveaway stand out from others in your industry?
- How can you use a social media contest or giveaway to gather valuable customer data and insights?
- What are some ways to create urgency and encourage participation in your social media contest or giveaway?
- How can you use social media analytics to track the success of your contest or giveaway?
- How can you use gamification elements to make your social media contest or giveaway more interactive and engaging?
- What are some best practices for announcing and promoting the winner(s) of your social media contest or giveaway?
- How can you use a social media contest or giveaway to build and strengthen relationships with your followers and customers?
- How can you use a social media contest or giveaway to boost brand awareness and visibility?
- How can you use a social media contest or giveaway to promote a new product or service?

- How can you use a social media contest or giveaway to generate user-generated content (UGC) for your brand?
- What are some ways to tailor your social media contest or giveaway to specific social media platforms?
- How can you use a social media contest or giveaway to drive website traffic and conversions?

User-Generated Content (UGC) Campaigns

User-generated content (UGC) campaigns on social media are marketing strategies that involve encouraging users to create and share content related to a brand, product, or service.

This content is then shared on social media platforms, increasing engagement and promoting brand awareness.

Examples of UGC can include user- submitted photos, videos, or reviews.

The goal is to foster a sense of community around the brand, promote engagement, and increase user-generated content related to the campaign.

Prompts

- What is user-generated content (UGC) and why is it valuable for social media marketing?
- How can you encourage your audience to create and share UGC on social media?
- What are some effective ways to curate and showcase UGC on your social media channels?
- How can you measure the success of your UGC campaigns on social media?
- What are the legal and ethical considerations for using UGC in your social media marketing?
- How can you use UGC to build brand trust and authenticity on social media?
- What are the best practices for sourcing and using UGC in your social media campaigns?
- How can you incorporate UGC into your social media advertising strategy?
- What are the different types of UGC campaigns you can run on social media?
- How can you leverage UGC to increase engagement and reach on your social media channels?
- How can you encourage your followers to tag your brand in their UGC on social media?

- What are the potential risks and challenges of running UGC campaigns on social media?
- How can you use UGC to improve your product development and customer experience?
- What are some creative ways to use UGC in your social media marketing campaigns?
- How can you use UGC to personalize your social media content and connect with your audience?
- What are some examples of successful UGC campaigns on social media?
- How can you collaborate with influencers and brand ambassadors to generate UGC for your brand on social media?
- How can you use UGC to tell a compelling brand story on social media?
- How can you optimize your social media profiles to encourage UGC?
- What are some common mistakes to avoid when running UGC campaigns on social media?
- How can you use UGC to attract new customers and increase brand loyalty on social media?
- What are the key elements of a successful UGC campaign on social media?
- How can you use UGC to showcase your brand values and mission on social media?
- What are some effective ways to incentivize your followers to create and share UGC on social media?

- How can you use UGC to generate social proof and increase conversions on your website?
- What are some best practices for engaging with your audience and responding to UGC on social media?
- How can you use UGC to target specific audience segments and demographics on social media?
- How can you use UGC to create a sense of community and foster brand advocacy on social media?
- ▪ What are some ways to repurpose UGC across different social media channels and marketing channels?
- How can you use UGC to differentiate your brand from competitors and stand out on social media?

Social Media Customer Service

Social media customer service is the use of social media platforms to address customer inquiries, complaints, and feedback.

This involves monitoring social media channels for customer comments and responding in a timely and helpful manner. Social media customer service can help to improve customer satisfaction, build brand loyalty, and address issues before they escalate. It can also provide valuable insights into customer preferences and behaviour.

Prompts

- What are the benefits of providing customer service through social media platforms?
- How can you use social media to monitor and respond to customer inquiries in real-time?
- What strategies can you use to handle negative feedback on social media?
- How can you train your customer service team to effectively use social media for customer support?
- What tools and software can you use to streamline your social media customer service operations?
- What are some examples of successful social media customer service campaigns?
- How can you measure the success of your social media customer service efforts?
- How can you use social media to proactively engage with your customers and improve their experience?
- What role does social media customer service play in building brand loyalty?
- How can you ensure consistency in your social media customer service responses across different channels?
- How can you use social media to address common customer service issues and FAQs?

- How can you handle sensitive customer information on social media while maintaining privacy and security?
- What are some common mistakes to avoid when providing customer service on social media?
- How can you use social media to personalize customer service interactions and create a more engaging experience?
- How can you use social listening tools to identify and respond to customer service issues before they escalate?
- What role does social media customer service play in crisis management?
- How can you use social media to create a community of brand advocates who can provide support to other customers?
- What role do social media influencers play in social media customer service?
- How can you use social media to reward and incentivize customers for positive interactions and feedback?
- How can you use social media to identify and address customer pain points and improve overall customer experience?
- What are some key metrics to track when measuring the success of your social media customer service efforts?
- How can you use social media to turn customer complaints into opportunities for brand advocacy and loyalty?

Crisis Management and Social Media

Crisis management with social media is the use of social media platforms to address and manage a crisis related to a brand, product, or service.

This involves monitoring social media channels for negative comments, addressing the issues quickly and effectively, and providing timely updates to stakeholders.

Social media can be a powerful tool for crisis management as it allows for real-time communication with customers and stakeholders, providing an opportunity to mitigate the impact of the crisis and rebuild trust with customers.

Prompts

- What are some common types of crises that brands face on social media?
- How can a brand prepare a crisis management plan for social media?
- What are some key elements to include in a crisis management plan for social media?
- What are some best practices for communicating during a social media crisis?
- How can a brand monitor social media to identify potential crises?

- What role should social media influencers play in crisis management?
- What are some strategies for dealing with negative comments and reviews on social media during a crisis?
- How can a brand balance transparency and privacy during a crisis?
- How should a brand apologize on social media during a crisis?
- How can a brand rebuild trust with its audience after a social media crisis?
- What are some examples of successful crisis management on social media?
- How can a brand use social media to prevent future crises?
- What is the role of social media listening in crisis management?
- What are some ways to handle a crisis when there is limited information available?
- How can a brand turn a negative situation on social media into a positive one?
- What are some strategies for handling a crisis that involves sensitive topics or controversial issues?
- How can a brand use social media to address false information during a crisis?
- What are some examples of social media crises that were mishandled and why?
- How can a brand assess the impact of a social media crisis on its reputation?
- What are some ways to address internal communication during a social media crisis?

- How can a brand use social media to stay transparent during a crisis?
- What are some ways to manage emotions during a social media crisis?
- How can a brand create a crisis management team for social media?
- What are some ways to use social media to engage with customers during a crisis?
- What is the role of social media monitoring tools in crisis management?
- What are some common mistakes that brands make during a social media crisis?
- How can a brand use social media to prevent a crisis from happening in the first place?
- What are some ways to communicate with employees during a social media crisis?
- How can a brand handle multiple crises on social media at the same time?
- What are some ways to prepare for a crisis before it happens on social media?

A little note. Always remember to always use your own common sense with what you receive from ChatGPT.

600+ Chat GPT Prompts
for Social Media Marketing Success

Made in the USA
Middletown, DE
03 December 2023

43868151R00038